This notebook belongs to

_____

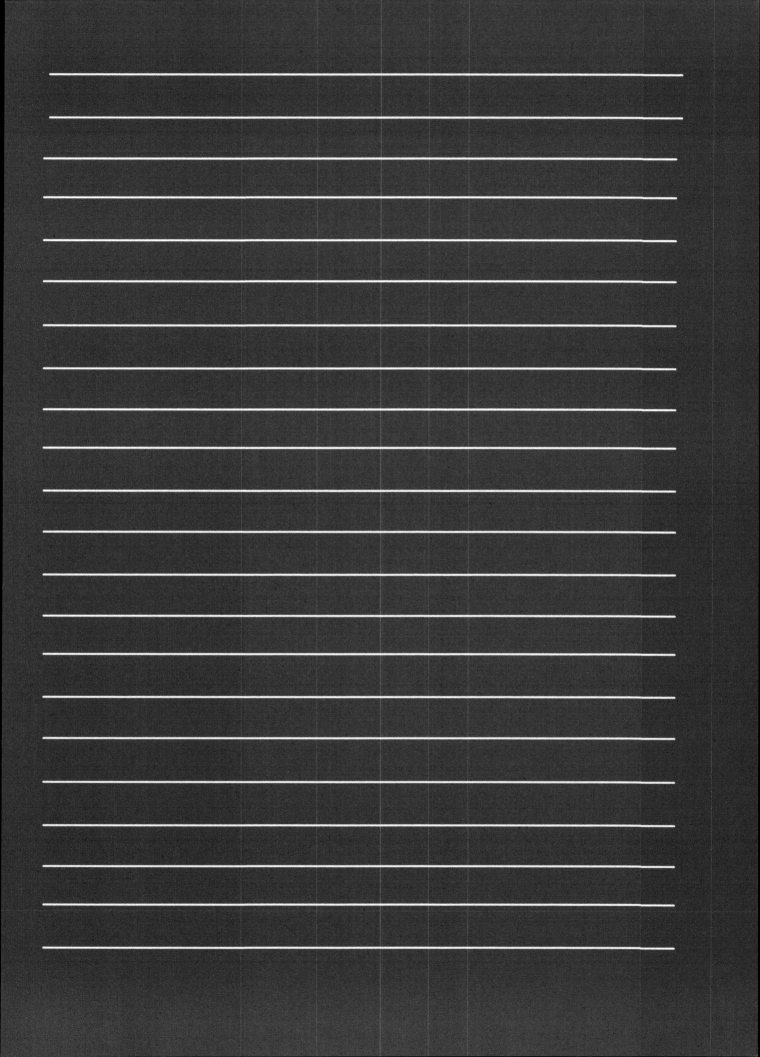

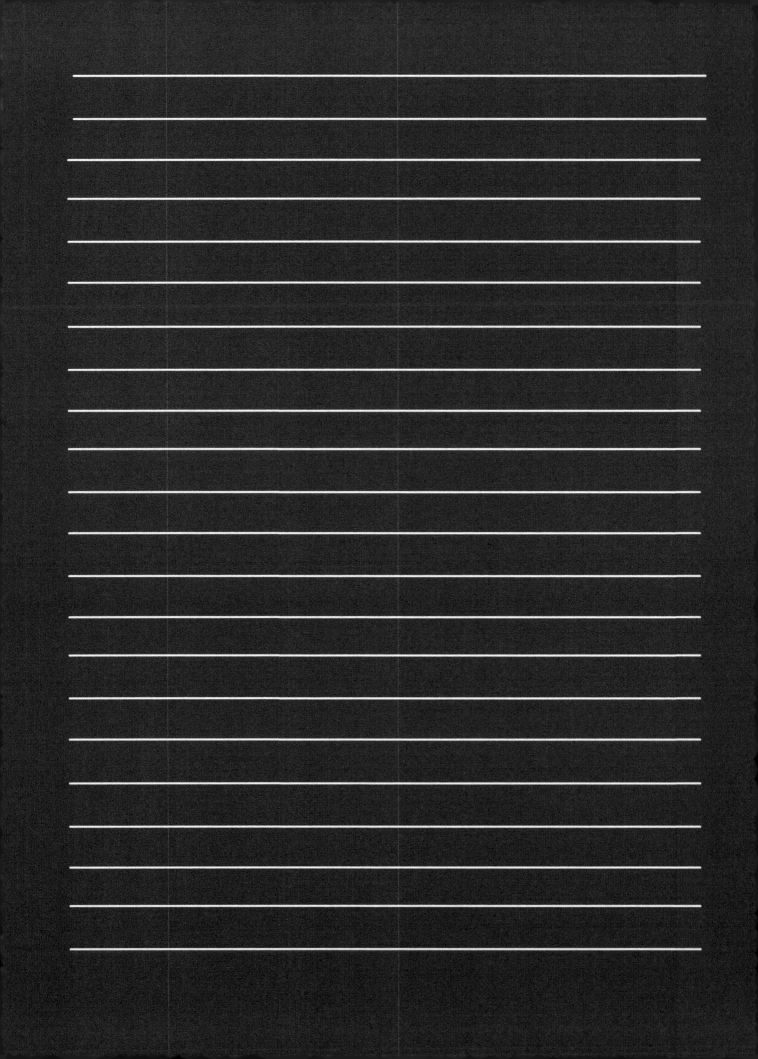

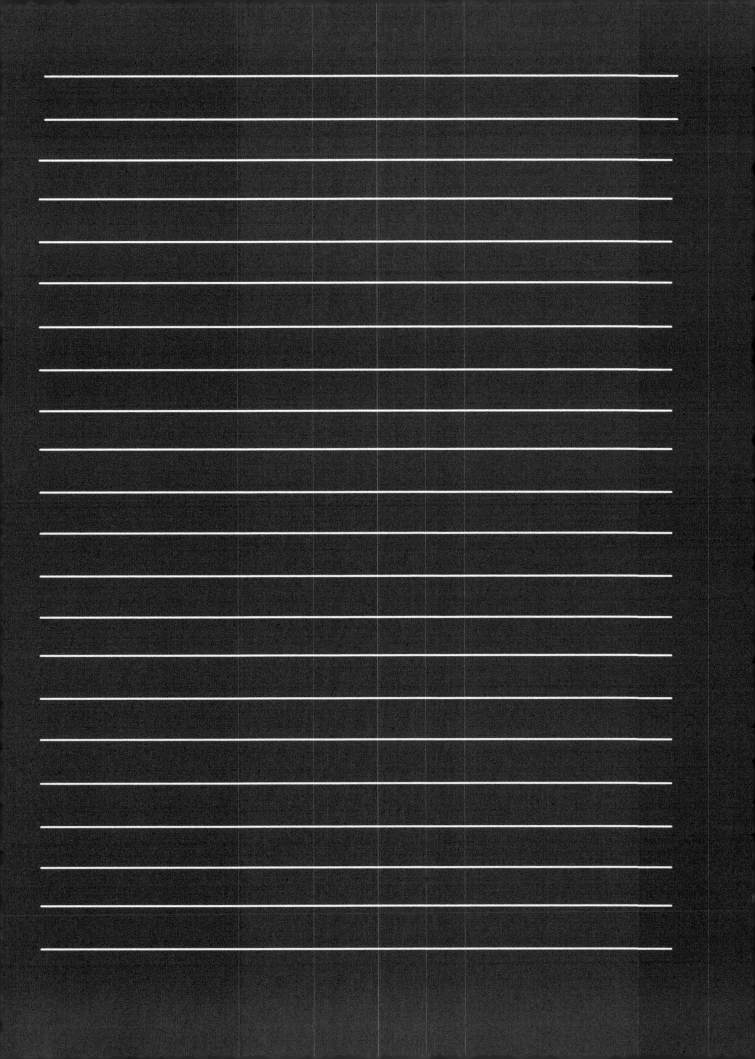

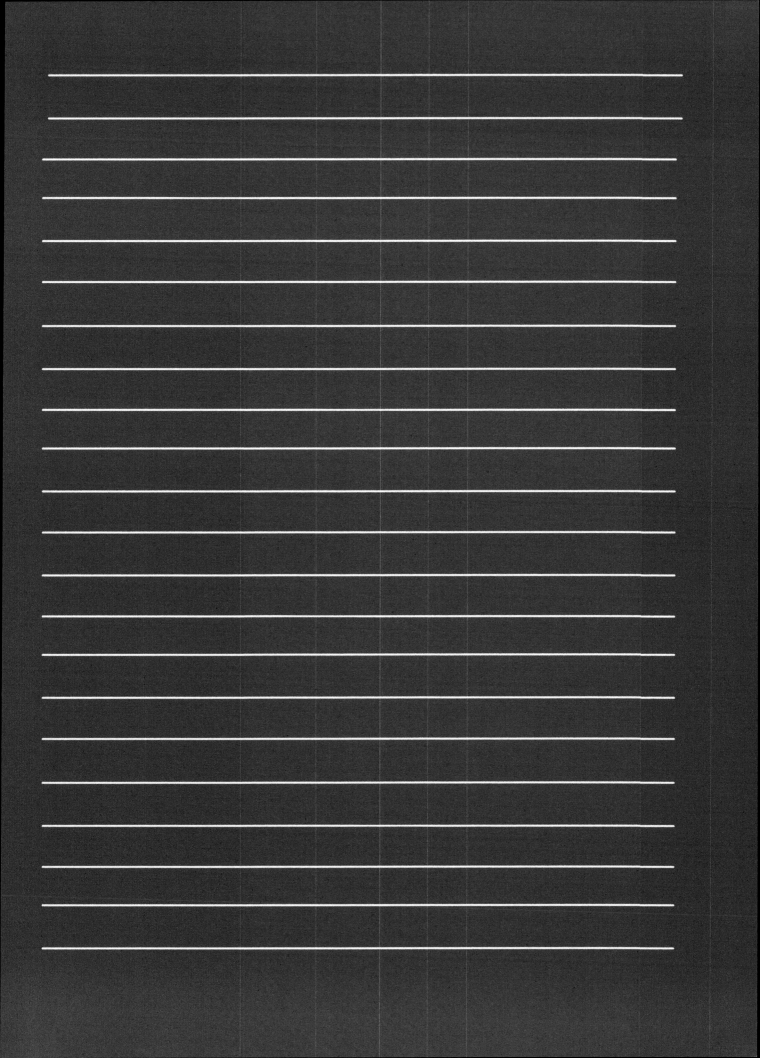

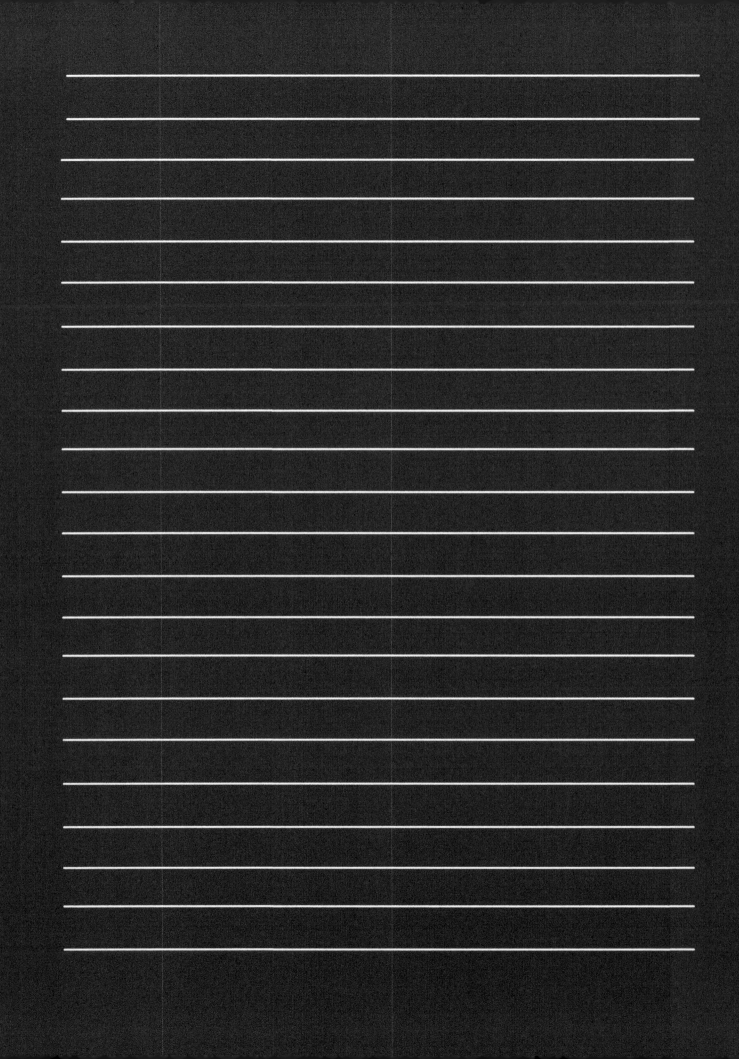

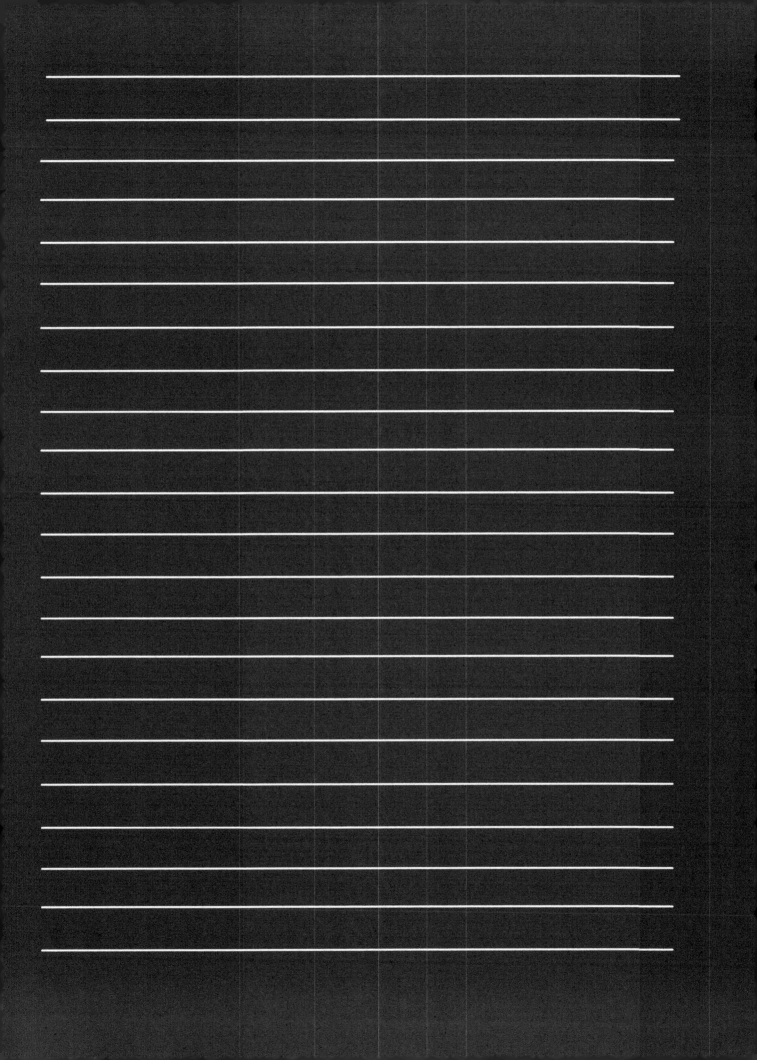

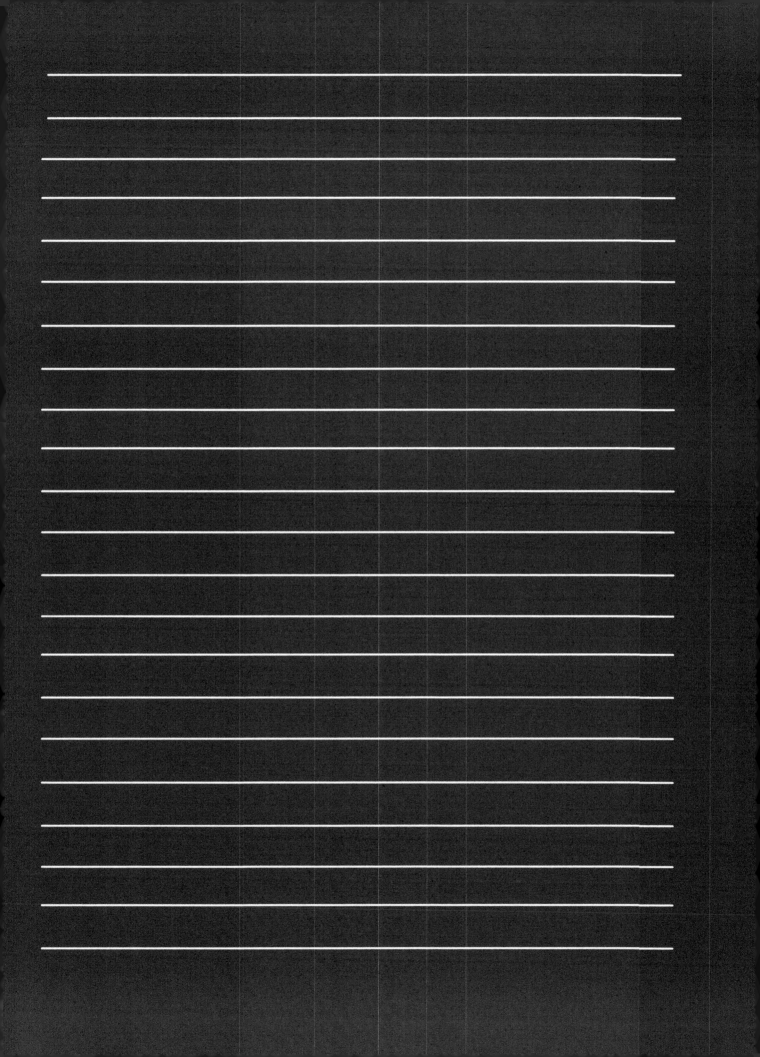

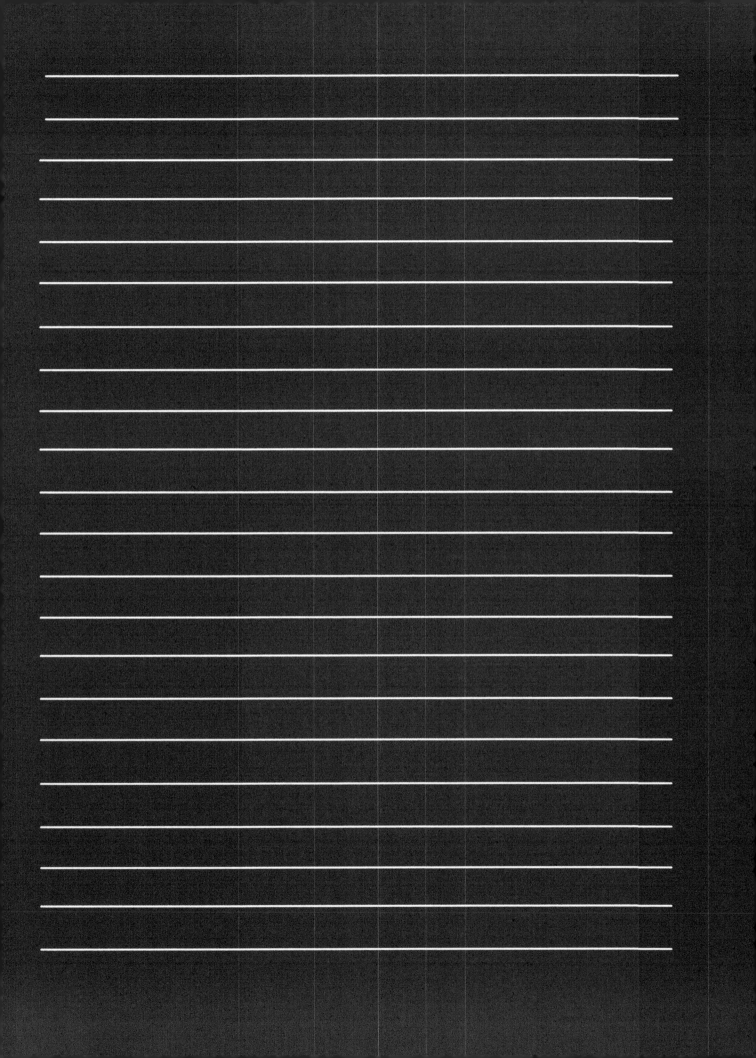

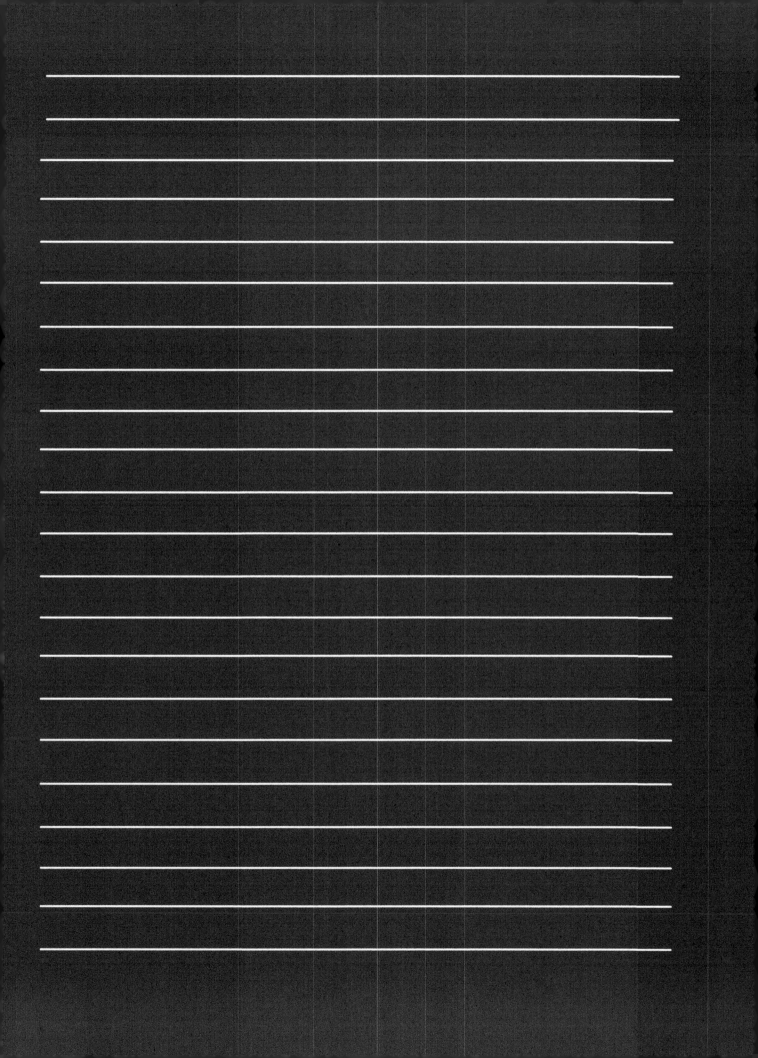

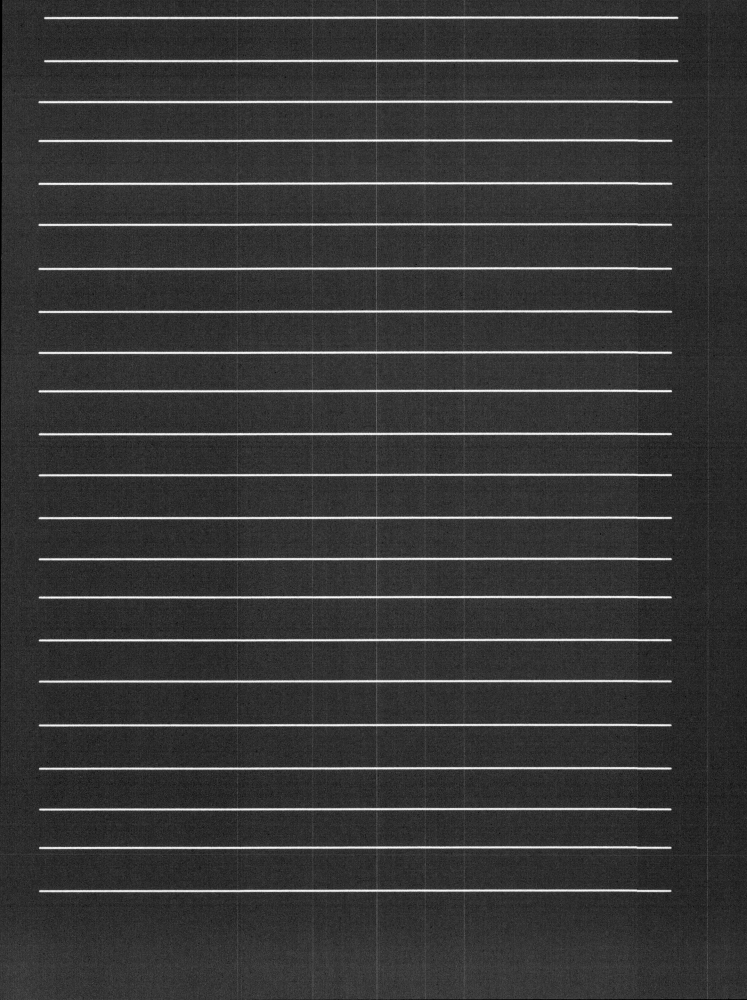

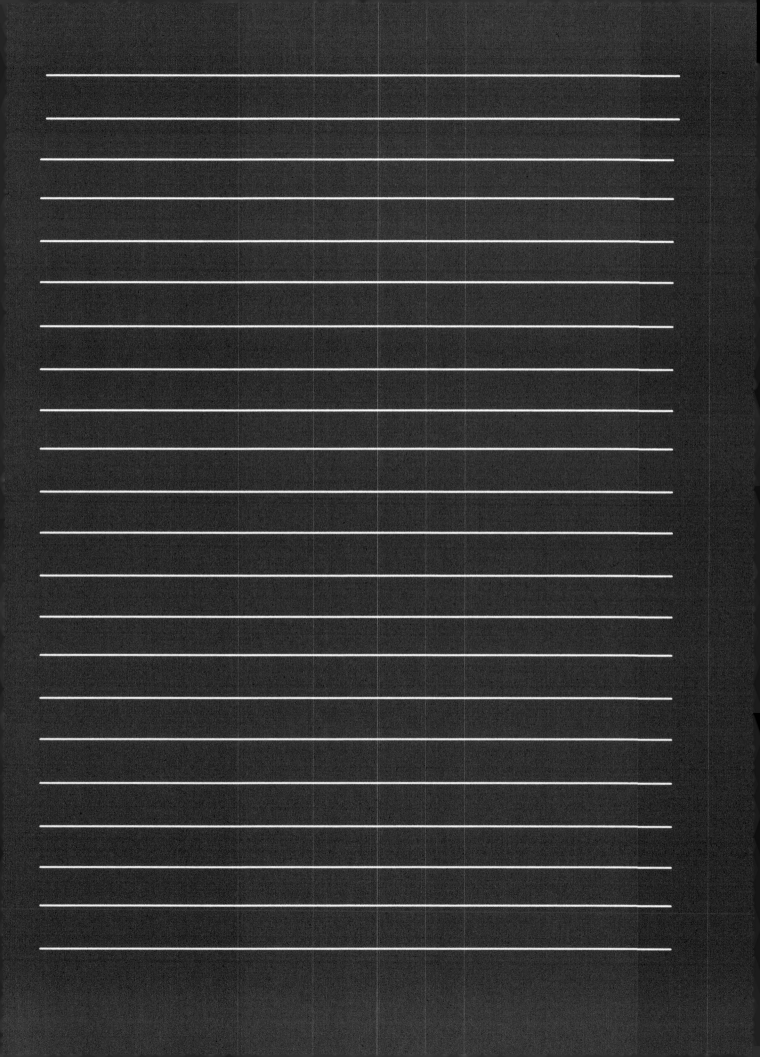

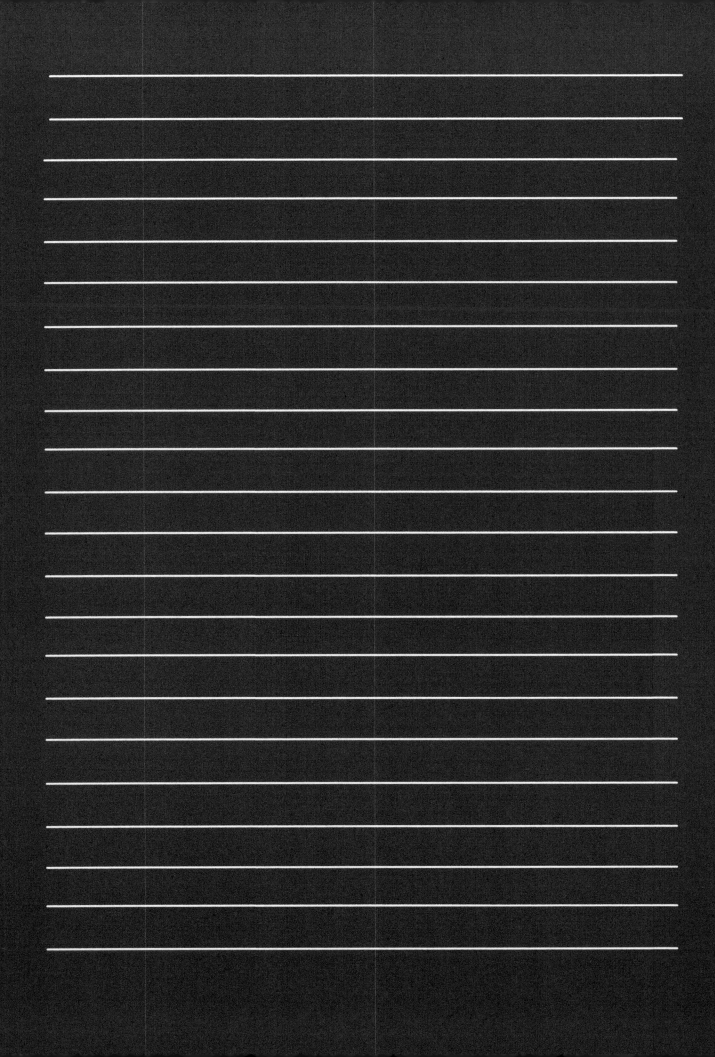

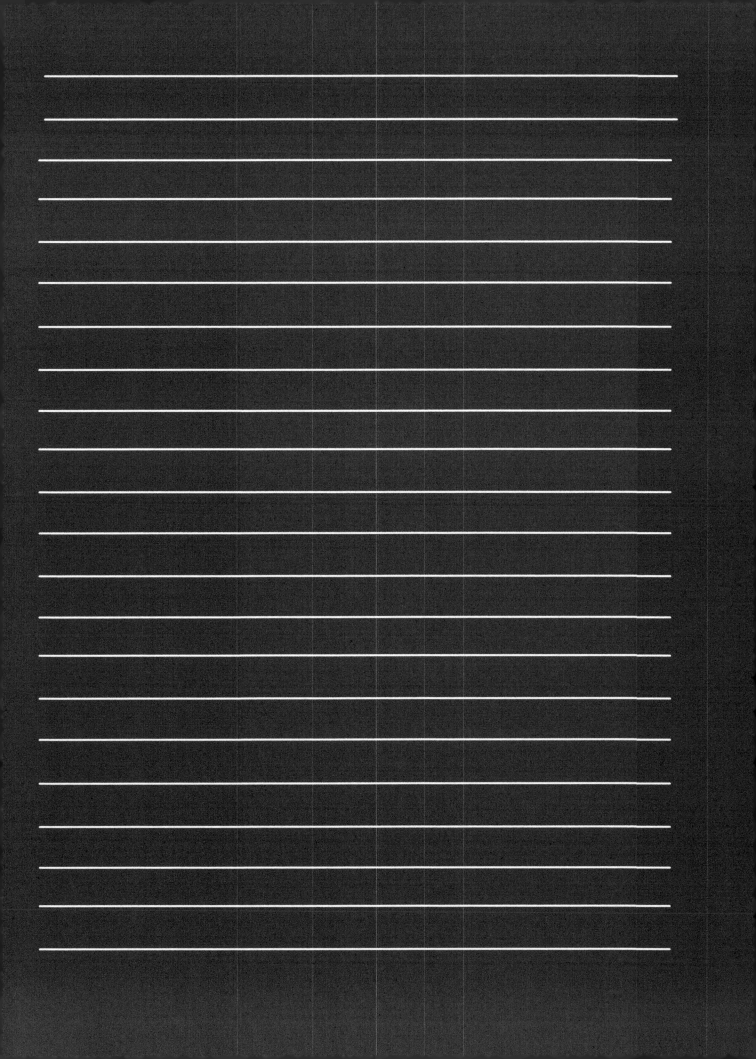

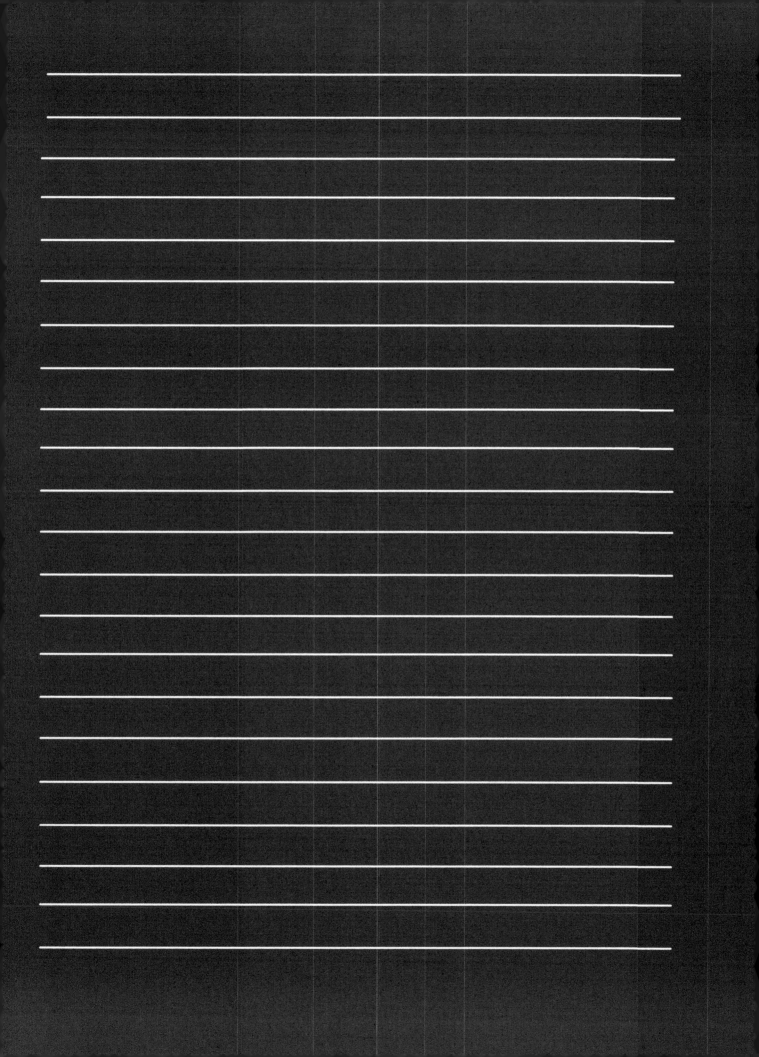

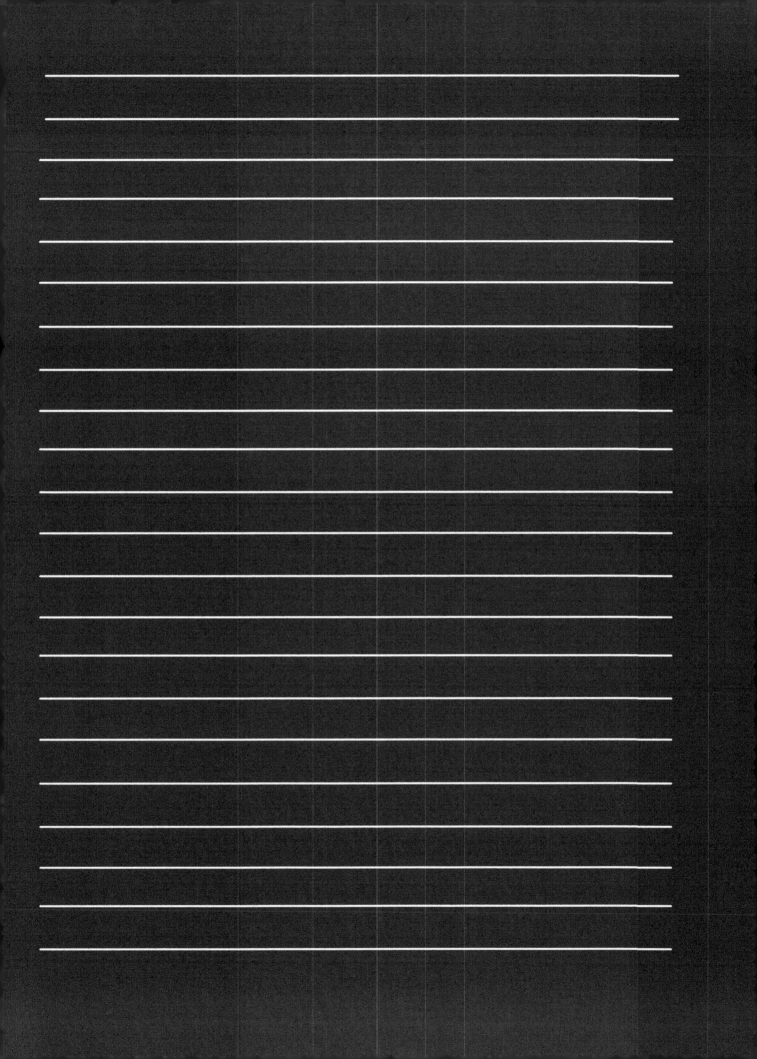

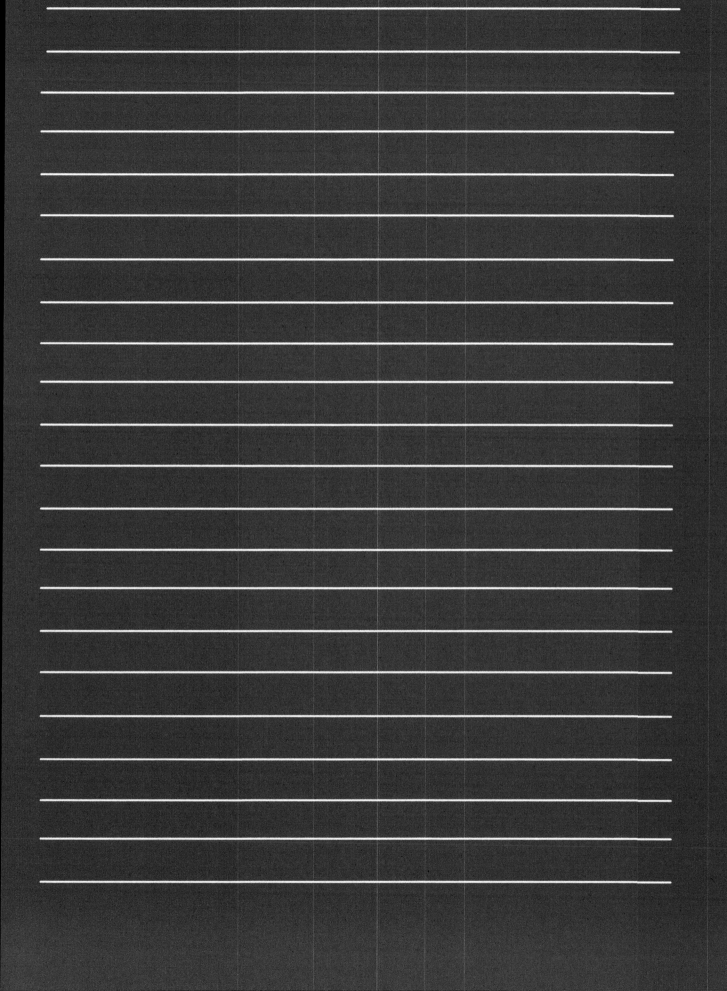

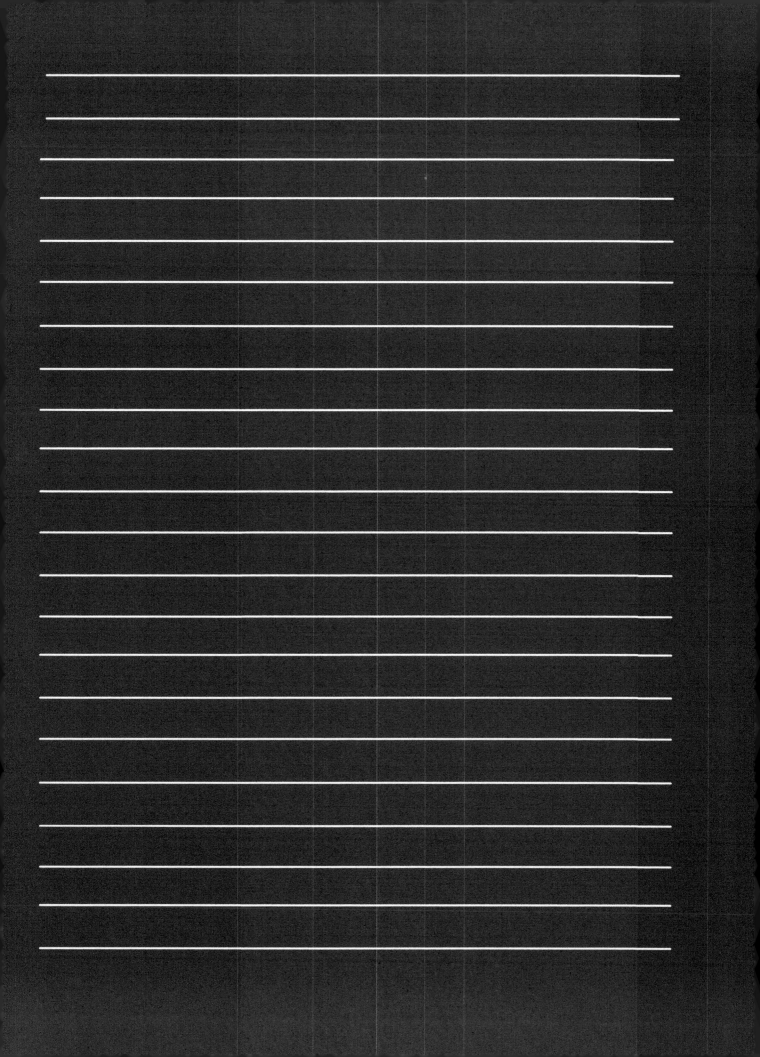

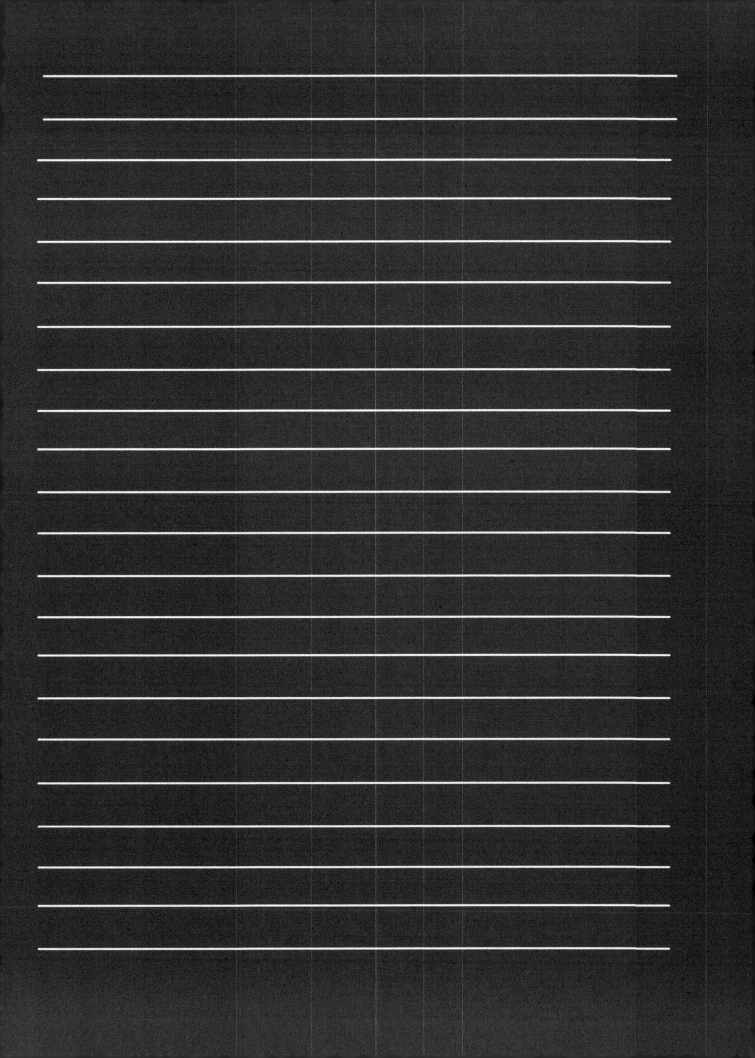

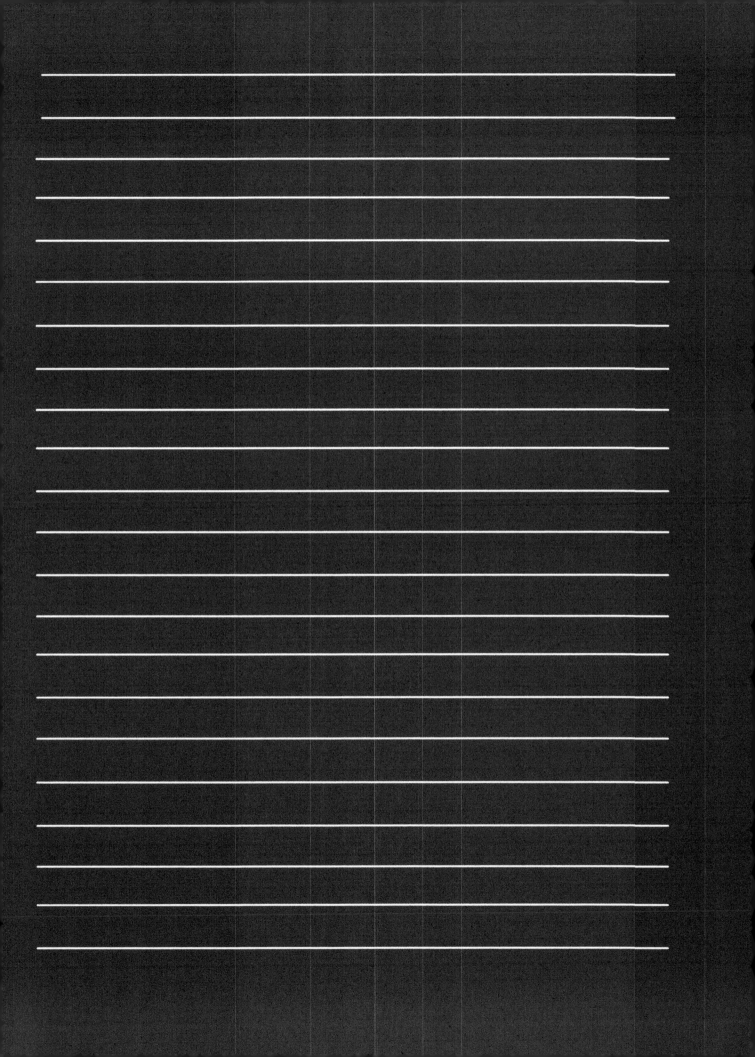

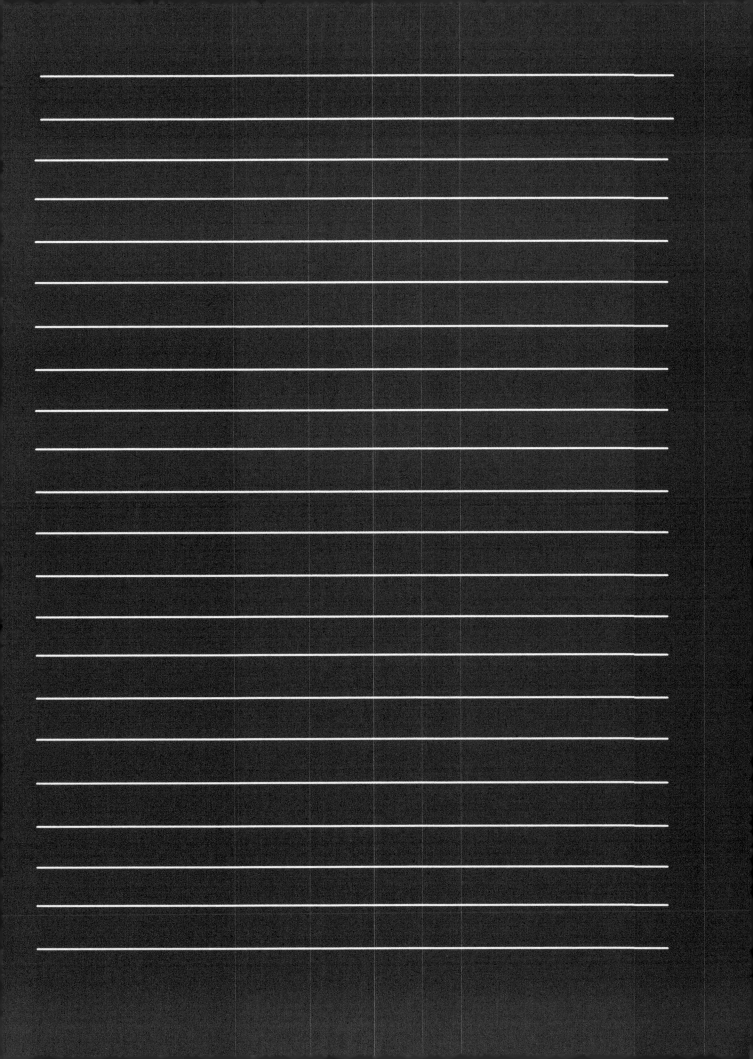

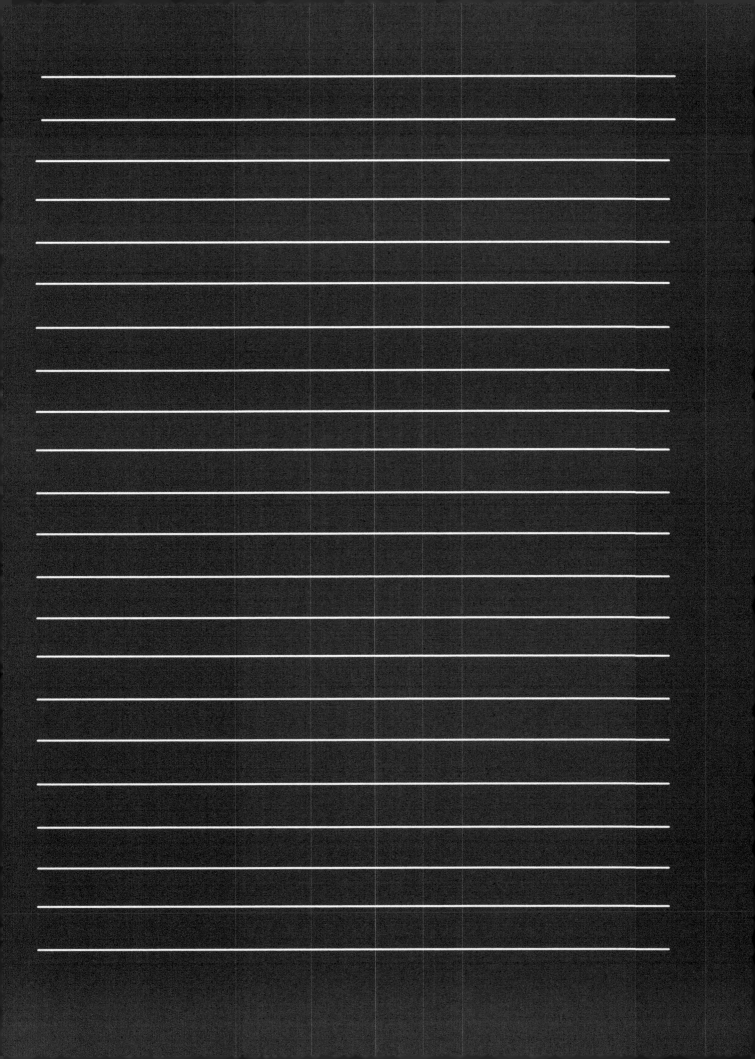

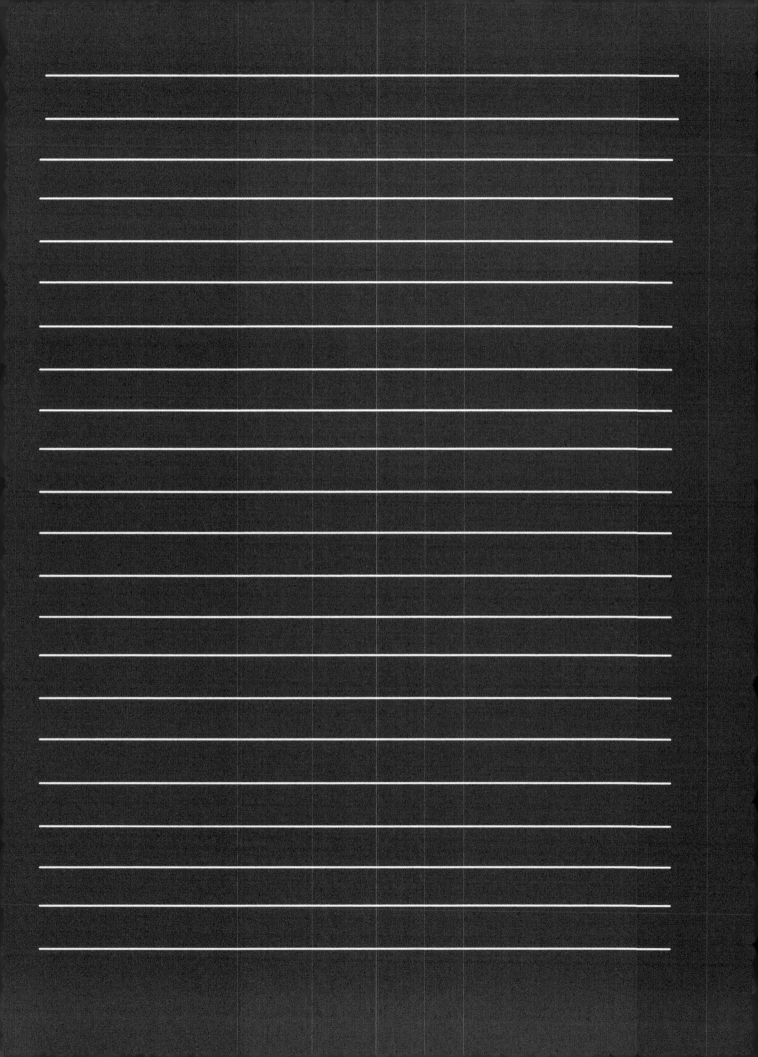

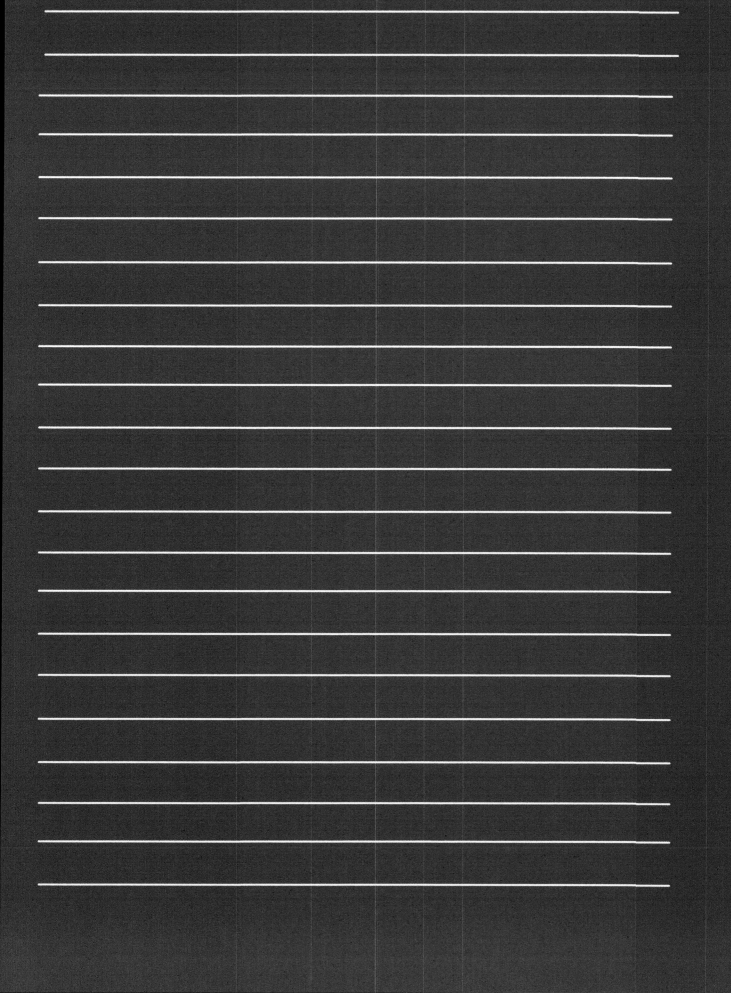

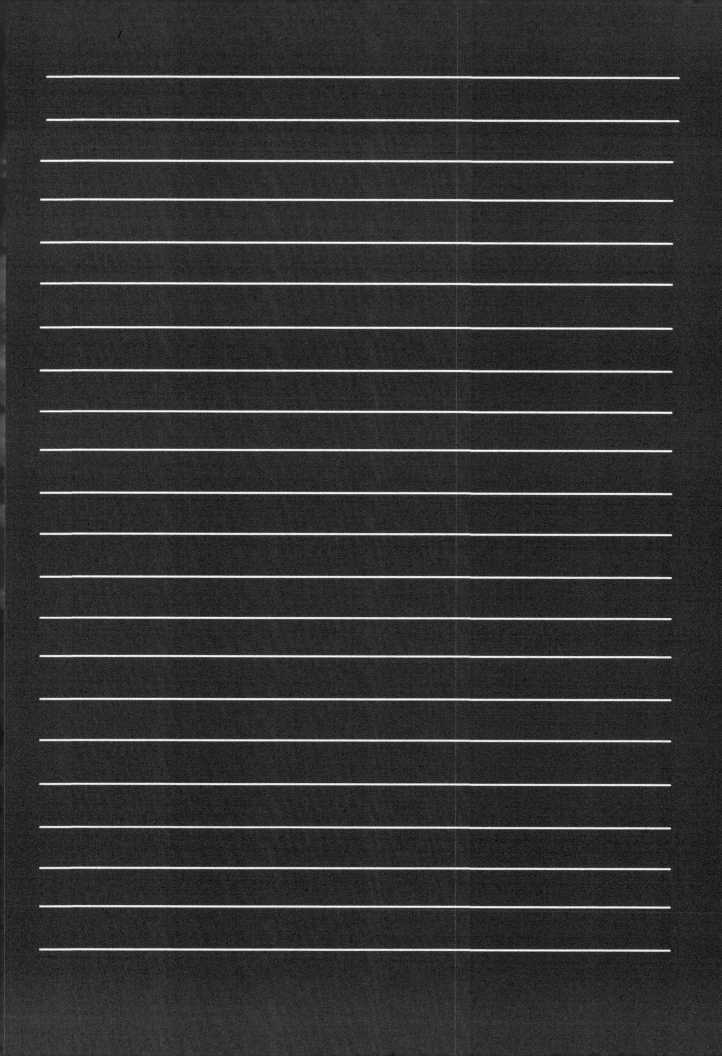

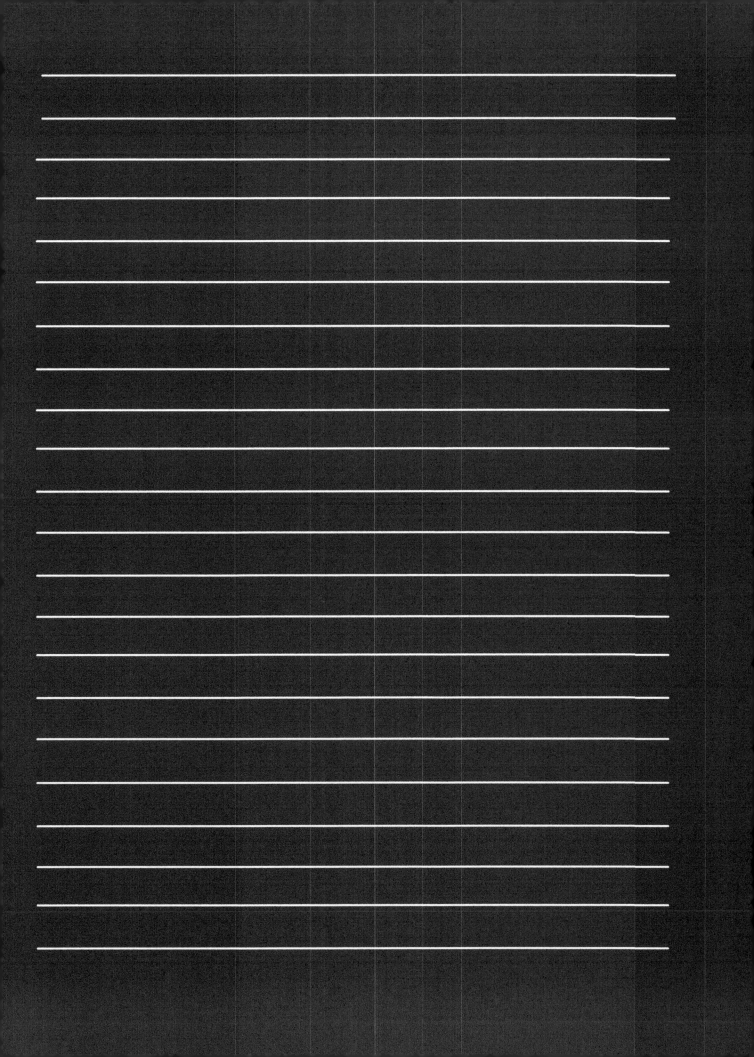

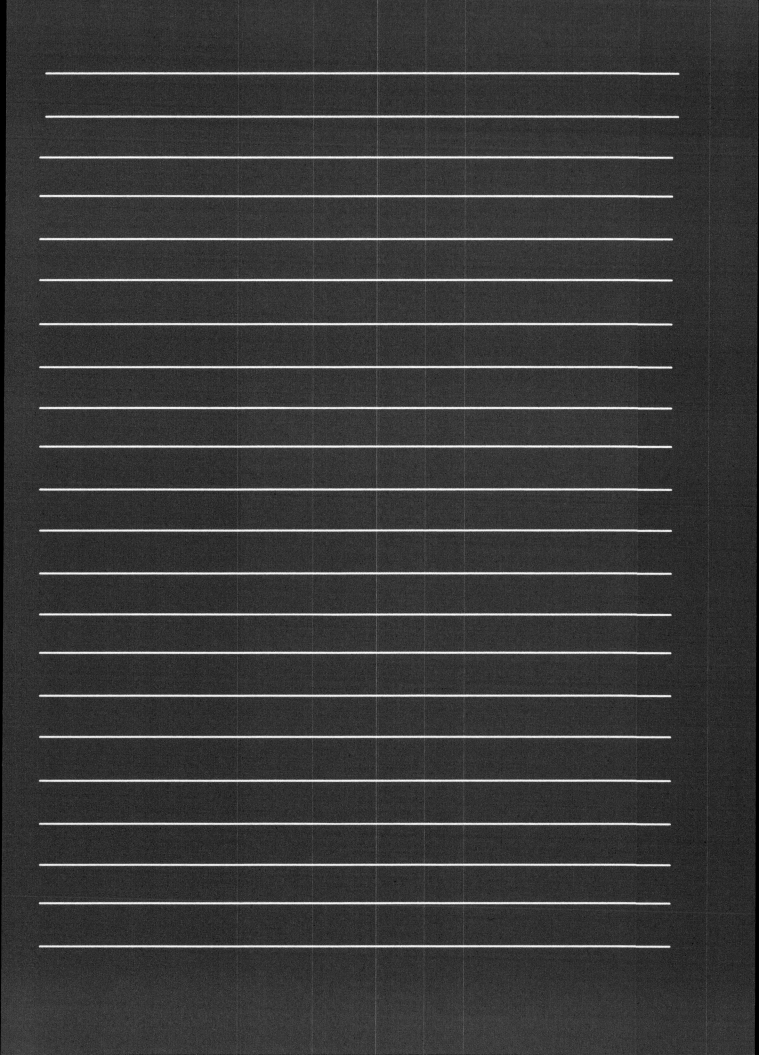

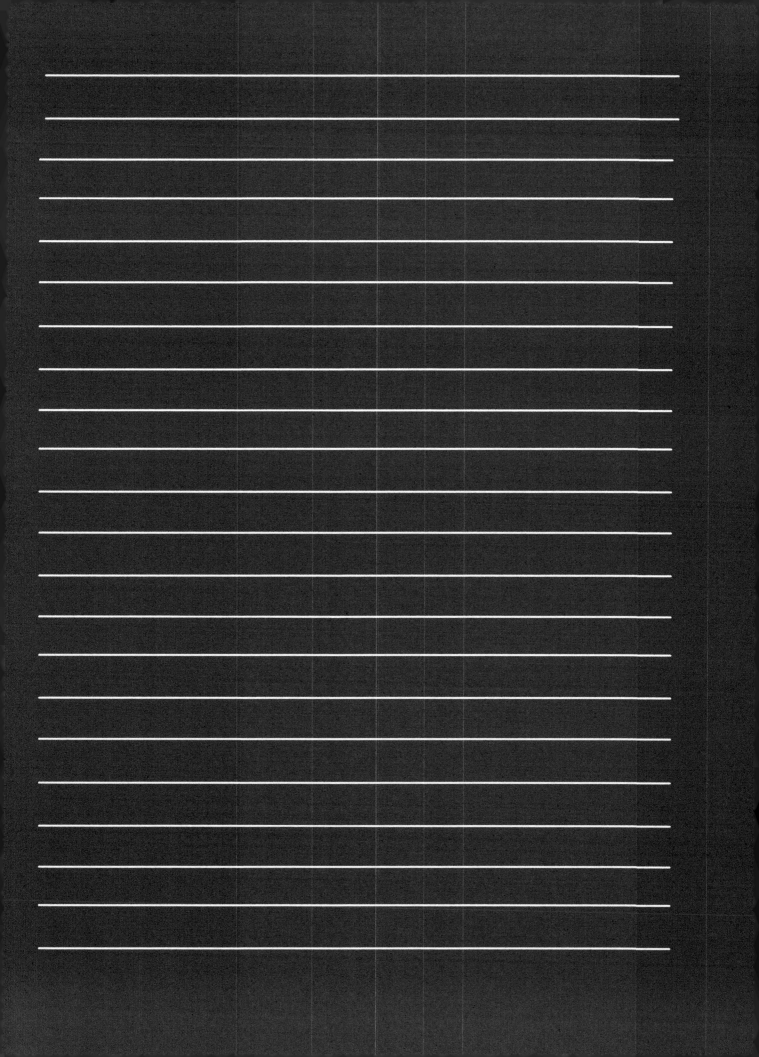

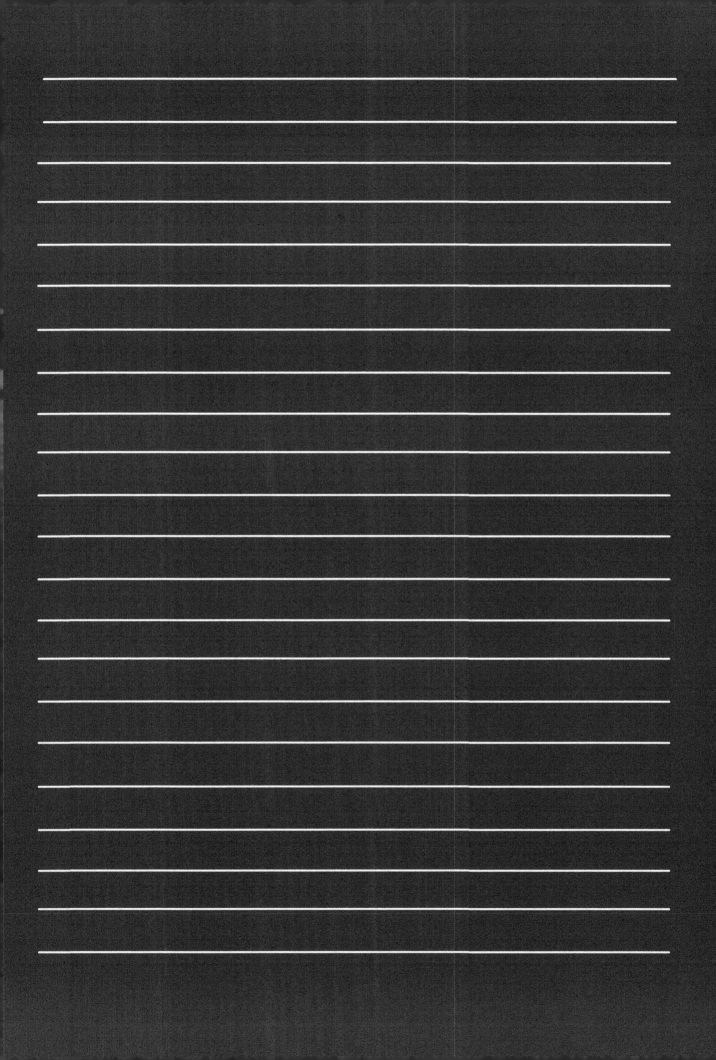

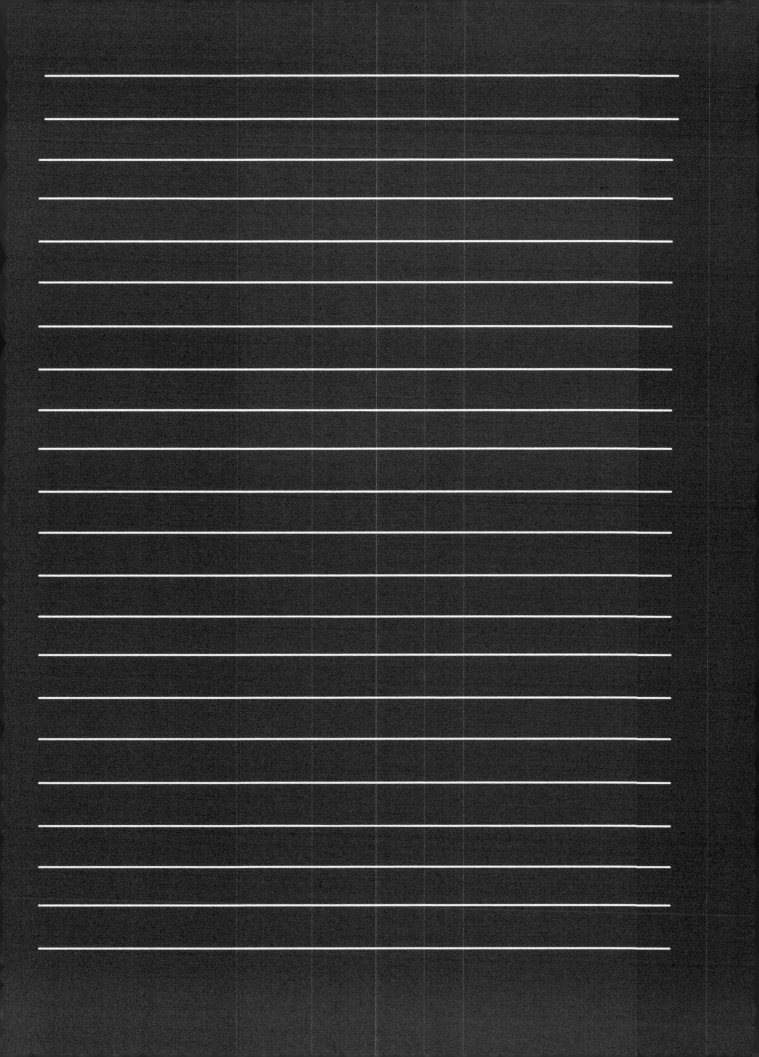

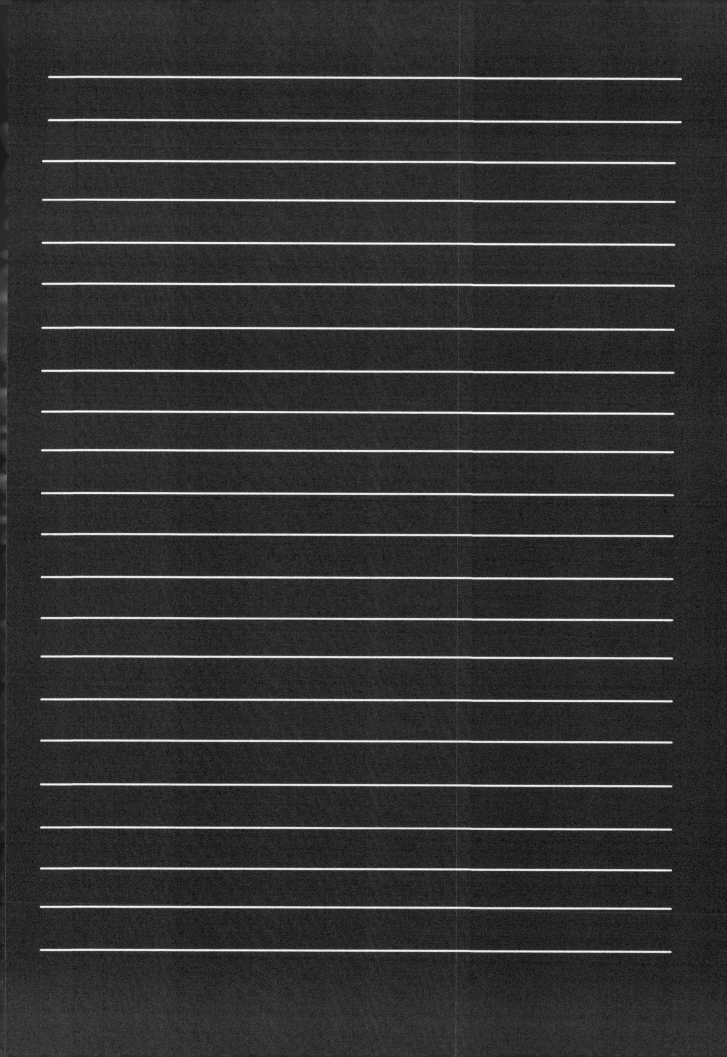

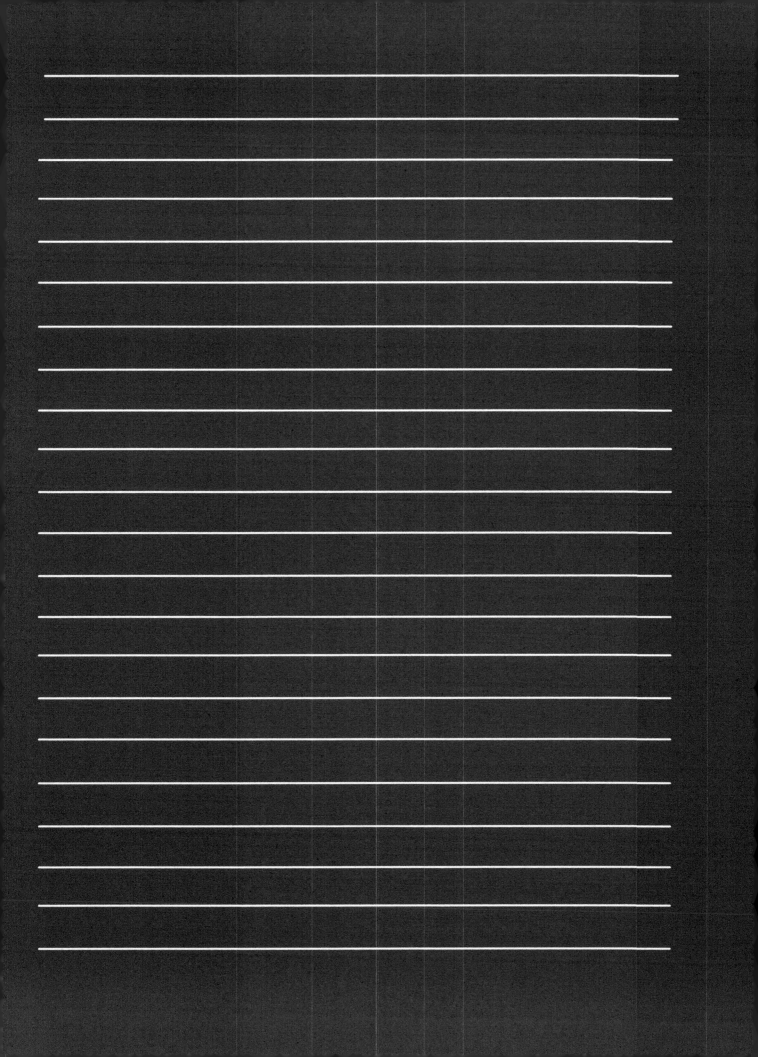

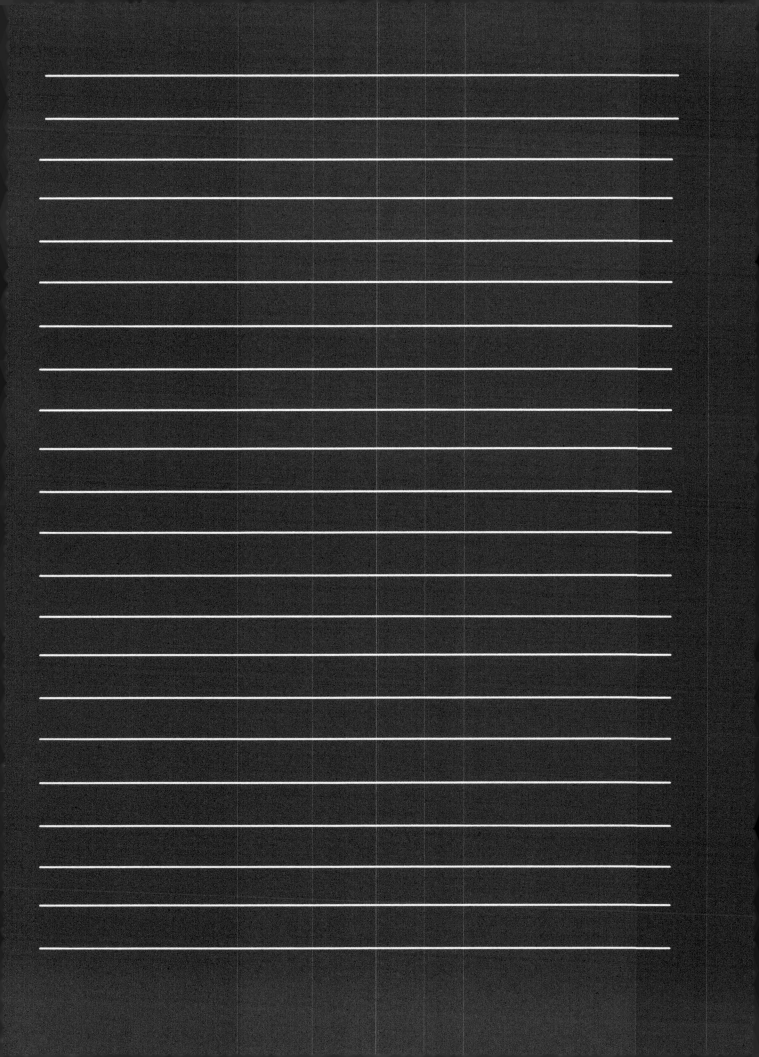

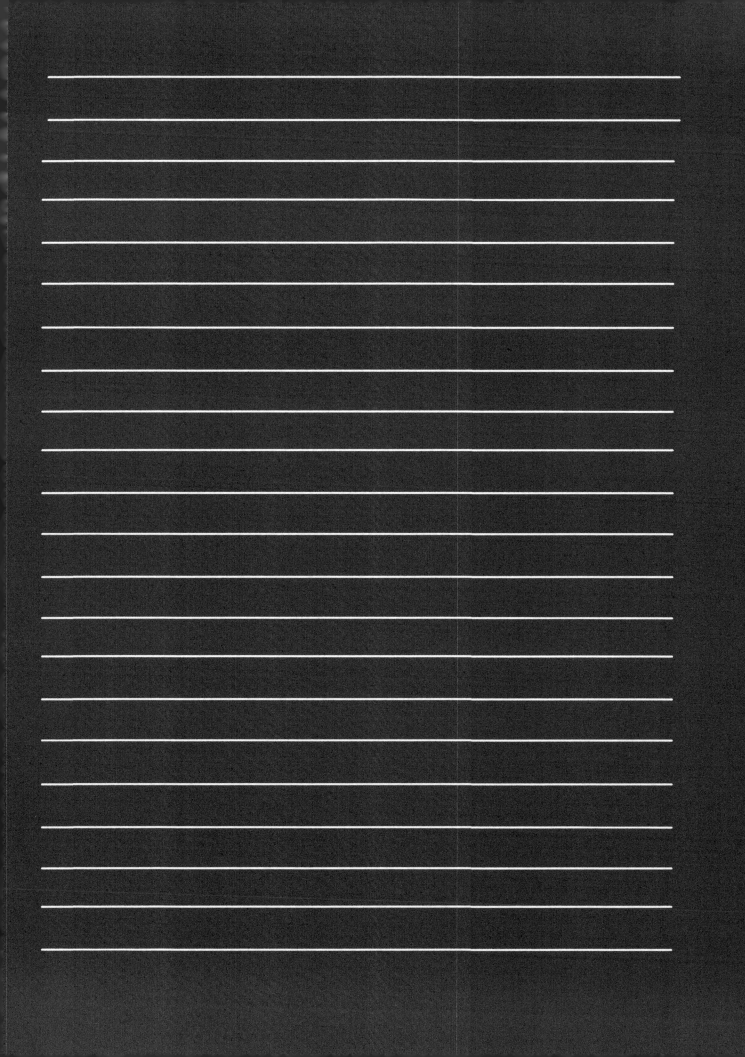

Thank you !

Purchasing this notebook helps
a new entrepreneur to achieve his
dream.
Because our goal is to deliver
quality over quantity, your
feedback is essential to us.
Please contact us at

costaopublishing@gmail.com

Thank you!

Made in United States
Orlando, FL
20 July 2024

49342773R00063